Science

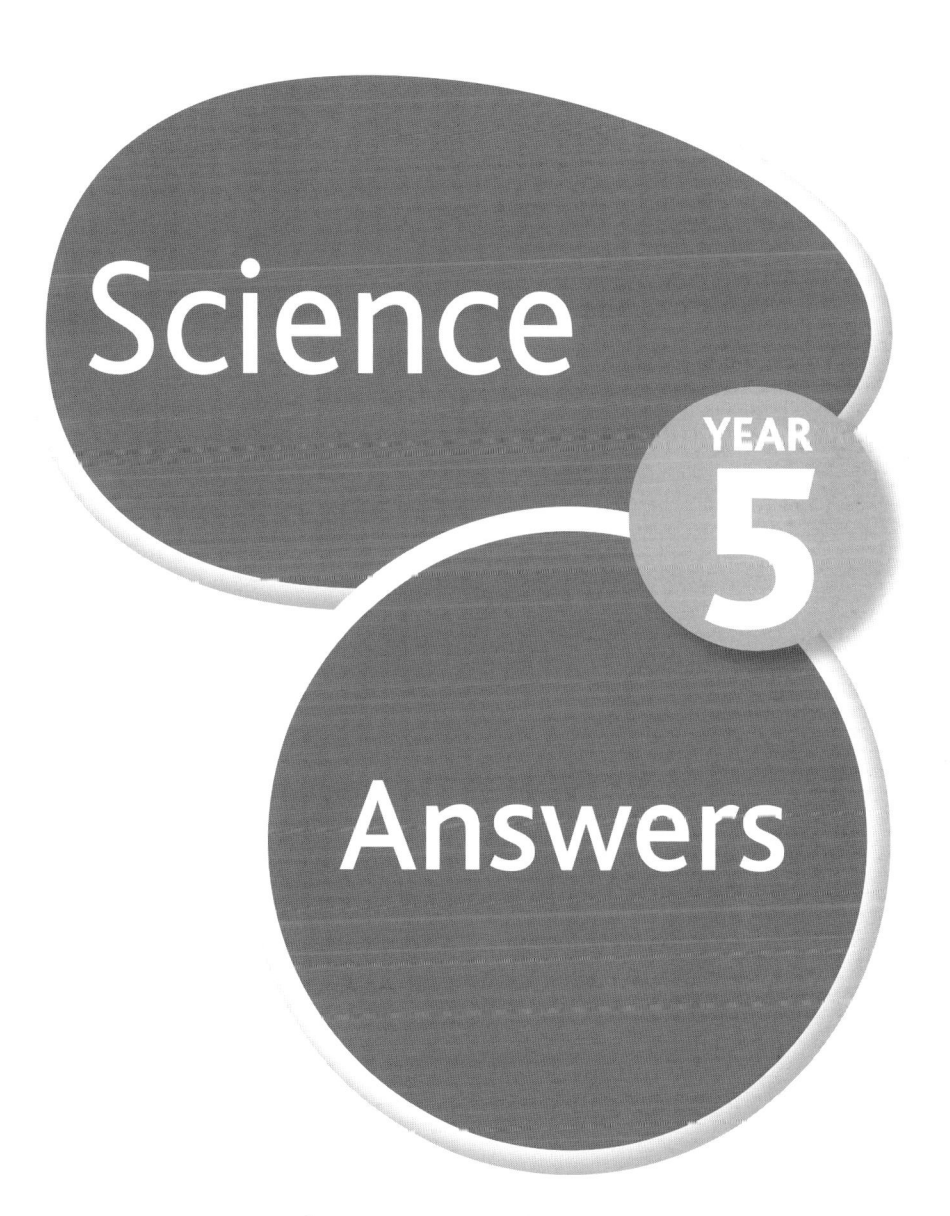

YEAR 5

Answers

Sue Hunter and Jenny Macdonald

GALORE PARK
AN HACHETTE UK COMPANY

Every effort has been made to trace all copyright holders, but if any have been inadvertently overlooked the publishers will be pleased to make the necessary arrangements at the first opportunity.

Although every effort has been made to ensure that website addresses are correct at time of going to press, Galore Park cannot be held responsible for the content of any website mentioned in this book. It is sometimes possible to find a relocated web page by typing in the address of the home page for a website in the URL window of your browser.

Hachette UK's policy is to use papers that are natural, renewable and recyclable products and made from wood grown in sustainable forests. The logging and manufacturing processes are expected to conform to the environmental regulations of the country of origin.

Orders: please contact Bookpoint Ltd, 130 Milton Park, Abingdon, Oxon OX14 4SB. Telephone: +44 (0)1235 827827. Lines are open 9.00a.m.–5.00p.m., Monday to Saturday, with a 24-hour message answering service. Visit our website at www.galorepark.co.uk for details of other revision guides for Common Entrance, examination papers and Galore Park publications.

Published by Galore Park Publishing Ltd

An Hachette UK company

50 Victoria Embankment, London, EC4Y 0DZ

www.galorepark.co.uk

Text copyright © Sue Hunter and Jenny Macdonald 2015

The right of Sue Hunter and Jenny Macdonald to be identified as the authors of this Work has been asserted by them in accordance with sections 77 and 78 of the Copyright, Designs and Patents Act 1988.

Impression number 10 9 8 7 6 5 4 3 2 1

2019 2018 2017 2016 2015

All rights reserved. No part of this publication may be sold, reproduced, stored in a retrieval system, or transmitted, in any form or by any means, electronic, mechanical, photocopying, recording, or otherwise, without either the prior written permission of the copyright owner or a licence permitting restricted copying issued by the Copyright Licensing Agency, Saffron House, 6–10 Kirby Street, London EC1N 8TS.

Typeset in India

Printed in the UK by Hobbs the Printers Ltd, Totton, Hampshire, S040 3WX

Illustrations Pages 16 and 17 by Ian Moores; other illustrations by the typesetter

A catalogue record for this title is available from the British Library.

ISBN: 9781471847561

About the authors

Sue Hunter has been a science teacher in a variety of schools for more years than she cares to remember. Her experiences have included teaching in a choir school and a local authority middle school, teaching GCSE and A level in the Netherlands and a short spell as a full-time mother of two. She was Head of Science at St Hugh's School in Oxfordshire until her recent retirement and is a member of the Common Entrance setting team. She has run a number of training courses for prep school teachers, including at Malvern College and for the Independent Association of Preparatory Schools (IAPS), and is currently IAPS Subject Leader for science and a member of the Independent Schools Inspectorate. She has also served for a number of years as a governor of local primary schools.

Jenny Macdonald has been a teacher for many years, teaching in both state and private schools. For the last 15 years she has been teaching science at St Hugh's School in Oxfordshire. She moved to Oxfordshire in the 1970s and has always enjoyed outdoor pursuits, having raised three children and countless chickens, sheep and dogs on the family smallholding. She is chairman of a local choral society, sings in a variety of local choirs, and would like to have more time to relax in the chairs that she enjoys re-upholstering.

Contents

	Introduction	vi
1	Life cycles	1
2	More about life cycles	4
3	Adaptation and habitats	6
4	Properties of materials	10
5	Reversible changes	12
6	Separating mixtures	14
7	Chemical changes	18
8	Earth and space	22
9	Forces	25

Introduction

About this book

Science is a subject that invites enquiry. The text in *Science Year 5* contains many interesting facts and opens the way for further research should a child feel inclined to find out more. Each chapter includes a number of exercises that are designed to focus the readers' attention on what they have read, assess their understanding of the material and to encourage them to think more analytically about the topic. There are a number of different types of exercise, for example cloze ('fill in the gaps') exercises, comprehension type questions and extension exercises requiring thought and application. All can be used in a number of ways depending on the ability of the pupils and the requirements of a lesson. The extension exercises, for example, could be used by teachers as stimuli for discussion, homework activities, opportunities for further development for quick workers and so on.

The answers given here should be seen as a guide. We do not expect every child to reproduce our answers exactly and each child should be encouraged to respond to the best of their ability. For some, success will be achieved if they can correctly extract basic information from the text. Others can be encouraged to look for more than the most basic answer by reading the text more critically. Those with the ability and interest can be encouraged to find out more and expand their knowledge through further reading or to think more deeply about the implications and applications of the material offered.

Sue Hunter and Jenny Macdonald

June 2015

1 Life cycles

This chapter covers the following elements of the National Curriculum for Year 5.

Pupils should be taught to:

- describe the differences in the life cycles of a mammal, an amphibian, an insect and a bird
- describe the life process of reproduction in some plants and animals.

Notes and guidance

- Pupils should study the work of naturalists and animal behaviourists, for example, David Attenborough and Jane Goodall.
- Pupils should find out about different types of reproduction, including sexual and asexual reproduction in plants, and sexual reproduction in animals

It also includes the following elements not mentioned in the National Curriculum:

- understand that fertilisation is the fusing of male and female sex cells in sexual reproduction (ISEB 1B).

Activities in this chapter offer opportunities to work scientifically by:

- comparing and contrasting the life cycles of different animals and plants.

Exercise 1.1

1 reproduce, extinct

2 cell, splitting

3 two

4 gametes

5 sperm

6 egg, ovum

7 gametes, fertilisation

Exercise 1.2

1 (a) germination

  (b) pollination

  (c) fertilisation

  (d) seed dispersal

2 Sexual reproduction involves cells (gametes) from two parents, one male and one female (and produces offspring that have characteristics of each parent). Asexual reproduction involves only one parent (and produces offspring that are genetically identical to that parent).

Exercise 1.3a

1 A complete change in body form during the life cycle.

2 (Red Admiral) butterfly, frog, moths (any two, accept valid alternatives)

3 nettles

4 Hard greyish-brown skin, inside a tent made by pulling leaves together and fixing them with silk.

5 Body shape changes from caterpillar to three-part insect, three pairs of jointed legs form on thorax, two pairs of wings develop.

6 Pupa skin splits, imago emerges and pumps blood into wings to extend them. Butterfly sits in sun for wings to harden before taking first flight.

Exercise 1.3b

1 metamorphosis

2 nettle

3 tents

4 pupa

5 pupa, imago

Exercise 1.4a

1 amphibians

2 in ponds (returning to the pond where they were born)

3 frog spawn

4 A tadpole has no legs, adult has four. A tadpole has a tail, adult does not. Tadpoles breathe through gills, adult has lungs. Tadpole lives only in water, adult lives mostly on land.

Exercise 1.4b: extension

1 (a) More eggs/tadpoles results in a lower chance of being eaten (accept other valid answers if clearly argued).

  (b) Greater competition for food and other resources.

2 In pools of water trapped in plants / in damp places, for example leaf litter / some carry eggs on their back or in their mouth (accept other answers if evidence from research is provided).

Exercise 1.5a

1. spring/March
2. cup-shaped, made from dead leaves and moss
3. four to six eggs
4. about 13 days
5. no feathers, eyes closed, (yellow rim to beak may be seen from photograph)
6. about ten days
7. insects
8. to leave the nest
9. They are not very good at flying so easily caught by predators.
10. Young robin is speckled brown in colour and does not have the red breast of the adult.

Exercise 1.5b

A robin's nest is made from **leaves** and **moss**. The female robin will lay about **four to six** eggs. The eggs are coloured **blue** and have **hard** shells. It takes about **13** days for the eggs to hatch. The baby robins have no **feathers** and their eyes are **closed**. The parents catch **insects** to feed the babies. When the baby birds' feathers have grown, they will leave the **nest** but they are not very good at **flying** yet. The parents will still feed them for about **three** weeks. Young robins are speckled **brown** in colour and do not get their **red** breast feathers for a few more weeks.

Exercise 1.5c: extension

1. A patch of land containing resources for feeding and breeding that is defended by an animal.
2. Good food supply, safe nest sites, resources for building nests, tall trees to sing from, bushy plants for shelter from weather/predators. (Accept valid alternatives.)

More about life cycles

This chapter covers the following elements of the National Curriculum for Year 5.

Pupils should be taught to:

- describe the changes as humans develop to old age.

It also includes the following elements not mentioned in the National Curriculum:

- how to compare different types of mammals, looking at the gestation periods (ISEB 2a)
- how the mass and length of a human baby changes as it grows (ISEB 2a)
- features of life cycles which are common to all animals (ISEB 2a)
- the physical and emotional changes that take place during adolescence (ISEB 2b).

Activities in this chapter offer opportunities to work scientifically by:

- taking measurements using appropriate equipment and units
- collecting data
- recording data in different forms
- looking for patterns in data
- researching information to answer questions.

Exercise 2.1a

1. Human babies need to learn how to feed, how to recognise their parents and how to tell them when they are hungry, tired or uncomfortable. They learn to smile, communicate and eventually to move around, play, feed themselves and walk.

2. Adolescence is the time when humans change from being children to being adults.

3. Boys' voices will become deeper and their bodies will become stronger.

4. A woman's breasts make milk for her babies.

5. A period is when the lining of the uterus comes away and the blood passes out through the vagina.

6. Boys and girls are both likely to become moody, they may develop spots and they grow more hair in places on their bodies.

Exercise 2.1b

1 sleep, care
2 adolescence
3 deeper, stronger
4 milk
5 uterus, month
6 moody, hair

Exercise 2.2a

1 Eggs are produced in the ovaries.
2 Sperm are produced in the testes.
3 Fertilisation is when an egg cell and a sperm cell join together to make one new cell.
4 The baby grows in the uterus.
5 A human baby takes about nine months to develop before it is born.

Exercise 2.2b

1 ovaries
2 testes
3 fertilisation
4 uterus
5 nine

3 Adaptation and habitats

Pupils should be taught:

- to identify how animals and plants are adapted to suit their environment in different ways:
- about the different plants and animals found in different habitats (ISEB 1c)
- how animals and plants in two different habitats are suited to their environment (ISEB 1c).

Activities in this chapter offer opportunities to work scientifically by:

- using appropriate techniques and apparatus during fieldwork
- paying attention to health and safety
- using keys and field guides for identification
- applying knowledge to make inferences and present reasoned explanations
- identifying and evaluating evidence used to support or refute an idea
- communicating findings clearly, presenting a reasoned argument.

Exercise 3.1a

1 The place where an animal or plant lives.

2 Food, water and shelter. A place where they can reproduce.

3 sunlight, water, space to grow, right kind of soil

4 community

5 (a) coast, farmland, rubbish tips

   (b) coast: fish
        farmland: worms and other invertebrates turned up by tractors
        rubbish tips: rubbish/waste food

6 adaptation

7 To move a long distance from one place to another to feed or breed at different times of the year.

Exercise 3.1b

1 feed, reproduce, shelter

2 community

3 anywhere

4 adapted

5 migrate

Exercise 3.2a

1. badger: sett
   red fox: earth
   squirrel: drey
   rabbit: warren

2. To spend the winter asleep/in a state where all body functions are reduced to a minimum.

3. bat (squirrels and badgers reduce activity but do not hibernate properly)

4. wood mouse, red fox, badger

5. excellent eyesight, hearing and sense of smell

6. To spot predators more easily to give more time to escape. (Accept valid alternatives if explained.)

7. active at night

8. bat, barn owl, wood mouse, red fox, badger

9. Owl needs to be able to see fast-moving prey from a long distance. Badgers feed in darker woodland and eat mainly less active prey and plant material so smell is more useful. (Accept valid reasoned alternatives.)

Exercise 3.2b

1. badger: sett
   red fox: earth
   squirrel: drey
   rabbit: warren

2. To spend the winter asleep.

3. bats

4. rabbits, wood mice, earthworms, blackberries (accept valid alternatives.)

5. To escape predators.

6. nocturnal

7. bat, barn owl, wood mouse, red fox, badger

3.2c: extension

1. Soft fluffy feathers on leading edge of wings stop the sound of the air flow over the wing.

2. (a) They emit high pitched squeaks which bounce off objects and return to their ears, allowing them to build up a sound picture of their environment.

   (b) echolocation

   (c) Not possible to see clearly for long distances because there is little/no light and the water may be cloudy.

Exercise 3.3a

1 Barnacle does not move; limpet moves across the rocks. Barnacle feeds by catching food through the top of its shell, using its bristly legs; limpet scrapes algae from the rocks.

2 Using strong threads.

3 To stop them from being swept away by the waves/tides. To make it harder for predators to eat them.

4 Has stinging tentacles to catch prey.

5 Can swim backwards. Can change its colour to camouflage itself against different backgrounds.

6 There is not enough light at these depths for it to carry out photosynthesis.

7 Shore crab has a hard shell; hermit crab uses cast-off shells from other animals.

8 Drop them from a height onto hard rocks.

Exercise 3.3b

1 sea anemone

2 mussels

3 herring gull

4 plankton

5 prawn

6 hermit crab

Exercise 3.3c: extension

1 The hermit crab collects sea anemones and sticks them to its shell. This helps to camouflage the crab and the anemone is able to feed on debris from the crab's food.

2 Advantage: the hermit crab does not need to use energy and resources making new shells at regular intervals. Disadvantage: the hermit crab's soft body is vulnerable if it is out of its shell changing from one shell to another.

Exercise 3.4a

1 (a) All mammals with fur, four legs, tails (and other shared characteristics). All are, at least in part, predators but with varied diets.

  (b) The red fox is reddish-brown all the year; the Arctic fox is white in winter but mottled brown in summer. The red fox is larger than the Arctic fox. The Arctic fox has smaller ears and shorter legs than the red fox

  (c) Its fur is not specially designed to insulate it from the extreme cold. It would also lose a lot of heat through its huge ears.
  (Accept valid alternatives to these answers as appropriate.)

2 (a) In early spring there are no leaves in the canopy so there is enough light to carry out photosynthesis and grow.

  (b) Frost damage, few insects for pollination.

  (c) Store food in the bulb and die back, remaining dormant until spring.

  (d) Thick waxy skin to prevent water loss. Leaves have become spines to stop them being damaged by heat and for protection from grazing animals. Photosynthesis carried out by stem. Water stored in the swollen stem. Ridges channel any water down to roots.
  (Accept valid alternatives to these answers as appropriate.)

Exercise 3.4b

1 predators

2 dustbins

3 rabbits, chickens, fruit, (any two)

4 two

5 lemmings

6 ears

7 leaves, sunlight

8 spines, eaten

9 water

Exercise 3.4c: extension

1 Labels could include: hump to store food, large stomach can hold up to 100 litres of water, do not sweat until body temperature is over 40°C, nostrils reduce water loss, long legs increase distance between body and hot sand, thick fur for insulation against heat and cold, long eyelashes and fur in ears to stop sand getting in, large flat feet spread weight for walking in loose sand.

2 Pupils will have individual answers that need separate consideration.

3 As above.

4 Properties of materials

This chapter covers the following elements of the National Curriculum for Year 5.

Pupils should be taught to:

- compare and group together everyday materials on the basis of their properties, including their hardness, transparency, thermal conductivity, and response to magnets
- give reasons, based on evidence from comparative and fair tests, for the particular uses of everyday materials, including metals, wood and plastic.

Activities in this chapter offer opportunities to work scientifically by:

- grouping materials according to observable characteristics
- planning investigations including identification of variables
- paying due attention to health and safety
- making predictions based on scientific knowledge and understanding
- paying due attention to accuracy and reliability when carrying out investigations
- recording observations and measurements in a variety of formats
- interpreting observations, looking for patterns in data and using these to draw conclusions.

Exercise 4.1a

1 what objects are made from

2 the ways in which materials behave

3 Accept any correct/plausible answer.

4 wood/steel/plastic/fabric, etc. as appropriate

5 light, not easily broken, does not form sharp edges, easily formed, cheap, can be coloured (accept valid alternatives), does not easily catch fire

6 transparent (accept valid alternatives)

7 (a) for example, transparent perspex/plastic

   (b) advantages: lighter, cheaper, less brittle (accept valid alternatives); disadvantages: less strong, less rigid, easily scratched (accept valid alternatives).

Exercise 4.1b

1 materials

2 properties

3 glass, transparent

4 plastic, wood

5 plastic, light, break

Exercise 4.1c: extension
1 (a) Accept any valid suggestion.

   (b) as above

2 cheaper, easier to make, lighter, more colourful (accept valid alternatives)

Exercise 4.2a
1 (a) A: 0.9 cm, B: 1.8 cm, C: 0.5 cm, D: 1.1 cm

   (b) B

   (c) C

   (d) Yes. Same sized paper strips, mounted at same level so dipped into water at same level, left in for same time.

2 fabric/paper/card (accept valid alternatives)

Exercise 4.2b: extension
Stretch paper towels over equal sized beakers or containers and secure with elastic bands. Add equal quantities of water to each. Add masses to each until it splits. One that holds most is the strongest.

Accept any workable alternative that will give satisfactory results, clearly described with mention of what would be done to make a fair test and how the strongest would be identified.

Exercise 4.3a
1 walking and climbing

2 burdock

3 Seed cases have tiny hooks that became trapped in the fur.

4 seed dispersal

5 to make two strips of fabric, one with hooks and one with loops, to act like a zipper

6 thought it was silly

7 from the French words for velvet and hook

Exercise 4.3b
1 Switzerland

2 burrs

3 hooks

4 loops

5 Velcro®, velvet

Exercise 4.3c: extension
1 pupils' own answers

2 Individual advertisements need assessing on the accuracy of the information, clarity of writing with regard to target audience, presentation, sources of information, images and so on.

5 Reversible changes

This chapter covers the following elements of the National Curriculum for Year 5.

Pupils should be taught to:

- know that some materials will dissolve in liquid to form a solution, and describe how to recover a substance from a solution
- demonstrate that dissolving, mixing and changes of state are reversible changes.

It also covers the following elements not mentioned in the National Curriculum:

- describe changes that occur when materials are mixed (e.g. adding salt to water) (ISEB 3c)
- factors affecting the rate of dissolving everyday substances in water, such as the temperature of the solvent, particle size of the solute and stirring (ISEB 3d)
- how to take an investigative approach to separate a variety of mixtures (ISEB 3g)
- when physical changes (for example, changes of state, formation of solutions) take place, mass is conserved (ISEB 3h).

Activities in this chapter offer opportunities to work scientifically by:

- taking and recording measurements accurately using appropriate equipment
- observing and comparing changes in materials
- drawing conclusions from observations and measurements
- paying attention to health and safety.

Exercise 5.1

1 dissolved
2 soluble
3 cannot
4 solution
5 solvent, solute
6 suspension

Exercise 5.2

1 (a) water

  (b) copper sulfate crystals

2 Use hot/warm water, use small pieces of copper sulfate/crush the crystals, stir the mixture.

3 Tiny pieces of an insoluble material floating in a liquid.

4 (a) temperature

  (b) volume of water, mass of copper sulfate, size of copper sulfate crystals, amount of stirring

  (c) The hotter the water, the faster the crystals dissolve.

Exercise 5.3a

1 The hotter the water, the faster the solute dissolved.

2 solute A

3 38–39 g

4 (see bar chart)

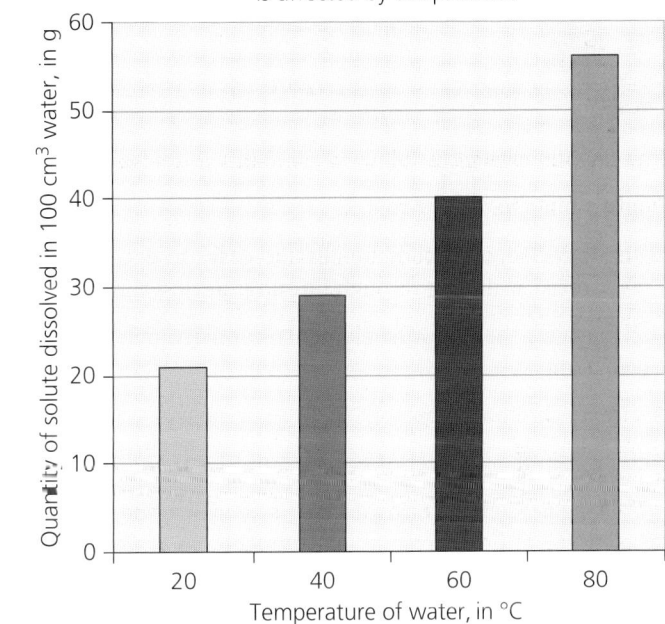

Bar chart to show how solubility of solute B is affected by temperature

(Quantity of solute dissolved in 100 cm³ water, in g vs Temperature of water, in °C: 20→~21, 40→~29, 60→~40, 80→~56)

Exercise 5.3b: extension

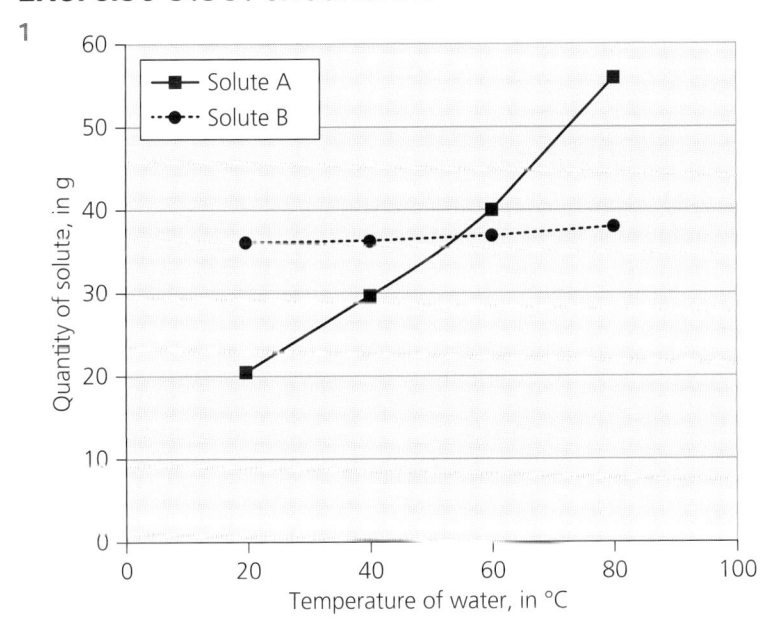

1 (Graph of Solute A and Solute B: Quantity of solute, in g vs Temperature of water, in °C)

2 (a) 55°C

(b) 25 g

(c) 73°C

(Give credit for values correctly read from the graph as drawn, with construction lines shown on the graph to show how values were read.)

3 74 g (37 g in 100cm³ so 2 × 37 = 74 g in 200cm³)

6 Separating mixtures

This chapter covers the following elements of the National Curriculum for Year 5.

Pupils should be taught to:

- use knowledge of solids, liquids and gases to decide how mixtures might be separated, including through filtering, sieving and evaporating.

It also covers the following elements not mentioned in the National Curriculum:

- simple chromatography (ISEB 13+ chemistry).

Activities in this chapter offer opportunities to work scientifically by:

- making predictions using existing scientific understanding and experience
- using scientific understanding to select appropriate techniques in practical exercises
- using tables, charts and diagrams to record information
- recording data and results of increasing complexity using scientific diagrams and labels.

Exercise 6.1a

1 Two or more substances mixed but not chemically combined.

2 Nitrogen, oxygen, argon, carbon dioxide, water vapour (accept other named gases as appropriate). (N.B. hydrogen is not found in the air as it is too reactive/explosive).

3 No, proportions of oxygen, carbon dioxide and water vapour differ between inhaled and exhaled air/air may be polluted by gases from factories, transport, etc. differently in different places. (Accept other valid explanations.)

4 water, salts, algae/plankton, sand/mud, shell fragments, seaweed

5 Evaporate equal volumes of each and show that there is more residue in the sea water than in the tap water.

6 sodium chloride

7 between Israel and Jordan

8 Very high concentration of salt dissolved in the water (makes the water more dense and therefore more able to support the less dense human body).

9 lowest place on Earth (c.400m below sea level)

Exercise 6.1b

1 mixture

2 gases

3 nitrogen, oxygen

4 sodium

5 pure

6 lowest

7 salt

Exercise 6.2a

1 liquid part of a solution

2 salt

3 Tiny pieces of an insoluble material floating in a liquid.

4 (a) decanting

 (b) evaporation

 (c) filtering

5 The dissolved salt would pass through the filter paper.

6 The hot crystals could spit out and the heat could change the solute in some way.

7 insoluble parts of the soil

Exercise 6.2b: extension

1 (Pupil answers are given in capital letters)

Material	Is it soluble?	Are the pieces larger than 2mm?	Is it magnetic?	Does it float on water?
Wax pellets	NO	yes	NO	yes
Powdered charcoal	no	no	NO	yes
Salt	YES	no	NO	NO
Iron filings	NO	no	YES	NO

2 Use a sieve to take out the wax pellets.
 Use a magnet to remove the iron filings.
 Add water to the remaining mixture.
 Filter to remove the charcoal.
 Evaporate the water to regain the salt.

Exercise 6.3a

1. Essential part of the diet, used for preserving food and trade.
2. (a) Sea water is trapped in shallow lagoons/salt pans and evaporated by the Sun.

   (b) Sea water is filtered then heated to evaporate the water.
3. Evaporation of shallow seas millions of years ago, interspersed with deposition of sediment from streams/rivers.
4. Bodies of dead sea creatures sank to the bottom of the sea and were covered by sediment. Heat and pressure from further layers of sediment changed them into oil.
5. tar, diesel, petrol, aviation fuel, plastics, candle wax, fibres for fabrics
6. fractional distillation
7. Oil is a non-renewable, finite resource and is running out. Burning oil products creates greenhouse gases, which cause global warming.
8. fuel made from plant material
9. Able to be made available continuously/renewable without damage to the environment.
10. Needs to be produced without cutting down forests or taking up farmland needed for food production.

Exercise 6.3b

1. preserve, meat
2. glass, timber
3. sea, mines
4. sea, millions
5. petrol, plastics
6. biofuel, sustainable

Exercise 6.4

1. Neat diagrams copied from the text as follows, drawn with a sharp pencil and ruler, appropriate size.

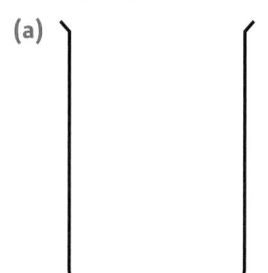

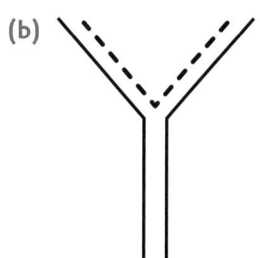

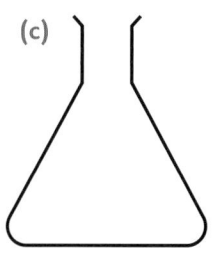

   (a) (b) (c)

2 As above but drawn from memory

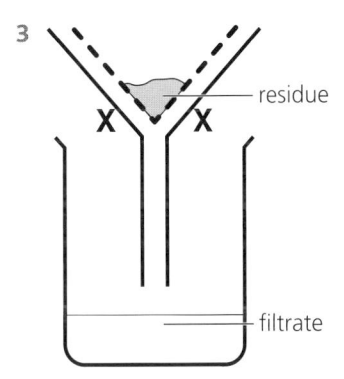

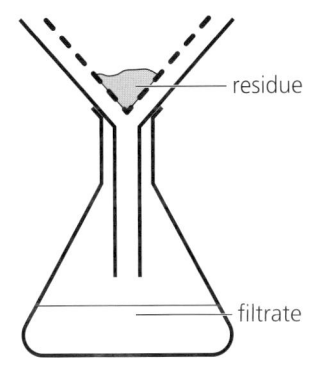

3

Exercise 6.5

1 Separation of a mixture of dissolved materials, often coloured, usually by the action of water or another solvent travelling up absorbent paper.

2 Art world: determining what pigments are present in paint. Forensics: analysis of paint or ink samples

3 The result of chromatography, usually a piece of paper with separated colour samples.

4 at the top

5 insoluble

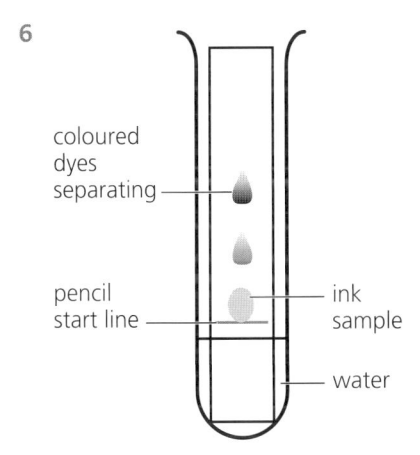

6

7 Chemical changes

This chapter covers the following elements of the National Curriculum for Year 5.

Pupils should be taught to:

- explain that some changes result in the formation of new materials, and that this kind of change is not usually reversible, including changes associated with burning and the action of acid on bicarbonate of soda.

It also covers the following elements not mentioned in the National Curriculum.

Pupils should be taught:

- that virtually all materials, including those in living systems, are made through chemical change in everyday situations, (e.g. ripening fruit, setting superglue, cooking food) (ISEB 3k).

Activities in this chapter offer opportunities to work scientifically by:

- making and recording observations
- handling laboratory apparatus with due regard for health and safety
- interpreting observations and measurements to make predictions and draw conclusions
- identifying different types of investigation
- using a range of sources to find out information.

Exercise 7.1

1 reversible

2 non-reversible

3 non-reversible

4 reversible

5 reversible

Exercise 7.2a

1 combustion

2 air/oxygen, fuel, heat

3 coal, oil, gas

4 extinguisher, air

5 electrical, fat

6 carbon dioxide, heavier

Exercise 7.2b: extension

Individual responses will need assessment for accuracy of message, clarity of communication with regard to target audience, presentation, crediting of sources of pictures and so on.

Exercise 7.3a

1 The candle uses up oxygen during combustion. At least 15 per cent oxygen in air required for combustion. Flame goes out when supply falls below this level.

2 nitrogen, oxygen, argon, carbon dioxide, water vapour (any two needed, accept named alternatives as appropriate)

3 nitrogen

4 oxygen

5 carbon dioxide, water vapour

6 carbon dioxide

Exercise 7.3b

1 true

2 False. A candle in a jar goes out when there is not enough oxygen left to keep it burning.

3 False. In a burning candle the wax is the fuel.

4 true

5 true

6 False. Limewater is used to test for carbon dioxide.

Exercise 7.3c: extension

Weigh candle. Allow it to burn for a while, making sure that no melted wax is lost. Weigh again. New mass will be lower than the original so some has been changed into new products which have been lost (as gases into the air). The change is therefore non-reversible.

Exercise 7.4a

1 presence of oxygen (air) and water

2 by boiling the water

3 Float a layer of oil on the surface to seal it.

4 silica gel (or anhydrous calcium chloride)

5 steel contains iron

6 Rust is weaker than steel and crumbles easily.

7 (a) Paint would wear off as the chain moves round.

(b) regular application of oil

8 (a) Covering steel or iron with a thin layer of another metal, usually zinc, to stop oxygen and water from reaching the surface.

(b) Cleaned, often in a bath of hot acid, and then dipped into melted zinc.

Exercise 7.4b

1 air/oxygen and water

2 Rust is weak and crumbly.

3 (a) zinc

(b) galvanising

(c) stops air/oxygen and water reaching the surface

4 paint/oil/layer of plastic/keeping dry

Exercise 7.4c: extension

Individual responses will need assessment for accuracy of message, clarity of communication with regard to target audience, presentation, crediting of sources of pictures and so on.

Experiments included should be clearly described with expected outcome.

Exercise 7.5a

1 Materials that occur in a usable state in the environment.

2 stone, slate, wood, clay (any two, accept valid alternatives)

3 Materials created by mixing and/or heating raw materials resulting in chemical change.

4 glass/plastic/steel/ceramics (accept valid alternatives)

5 sand, ash and limestone

6 any five suitable suggestions

7 oil

8 Oil is a non-renewable resource. Creation of plastics uses a lot of energy. Plastics are harmful in the environment.

9 Sea creatures and birds mistake it for food.

10 Limited space for landfill sites/creates harmful gases/waste of finite resources.

Exercise 7.5b

1 natural

2 clay, useful

3 glass/plastic, man-made

4 plastic

5 plastic, sea, food

6 recycling

7 landfill

Exercise 7.5c: extension

Individual exercises need assessing on the accuracy of the information, clarity of writing with regard to target audience, presentation, sources of information, images and so on.

8 Earth and space

This chapter covers the following elements of the National Curriculum for Year 5.

Pupils should be taught to:

- describe the movement of the Earth, and other planets, relative to the Sun in the solar system
- describe the movement of the Moon relative to the Earth
- describe the Sun, Earth and Moon as approximately spherical bodies
- use the idea of the Earth's rotation to explain day and night and the apparent movement of the sun across the sky.

It also covers the following elements not mentioned in the National Curriculum.

Pupils should be taught:

- how the position of the Sun appears to change during the day, and how shadows change as this happens (ISEB 4b)
- the concept of a moon as a satellite, as shown by our Moon and the moons of other planets; that the solar system is part of the Milky Way galaxy, and that the universe contains many such groups of stars or galaxies; about the scale of astronomical distances (ISEB 4e)
- that objects are pulled downwards because of the gravitational attraction between them and the Earth (ISEB 4f)
- that it is gravitational forces which keep the Moon in orbit round the Earth and planets in orbit round the Sun (ISEB 4g)
- that the Sun and other stars are light sources and that the planets and other bodies are seen by reflected light (ISEB 4h).

Activities in this chapter offer opportunities to work scientifically by:

- using models to explain observed phenomena
- using a range of sources to find information
- presenting information in a variety of forms
- discussing how the work of scientists over time helps to develop and refine understanding and theories.

Exercise 8.1

1. stars, galaxies
2. Milky Way
3. constellations
4. astronomer
5. telescopes

6 Galileo

7 Moon

Exercise 8.2a

1 a star

2 about 150 million km

3 about 8.5 minutes

4 eight

5 Mercury and Venus

6 Mars

7 telescopes, probes/orbiters, rovers

8 Not so hot that water evaporates nor so cold that it freezes – meaning liquid water (essential for life) is present.

9 icy rings

10 It is too small.

Exercise 8.2b: extension

Individual exercises will need assessing for accuracy of information, clarity of writing as appropriate for target audience, sources of any images and so on.

Exercise 8.3a

1 When an object blocks the light.

2 opaque

3 midday

4 When the Sun is low in the sky (morning and evening) the shadows are long. They get shorter as the Sun rises higher towards midday and then longer again as the Sun sinks after midday.

5 sundial

Exercise 8.3b

1 shadow

2 long, short

3 gnomon

4 Sun

Exercise 8.4a

1 nitrogen and oxygen

2

[Diagram: Sun emitting light from the Sun towards Earth. Earth rotates (spins) on its axis. The side of the Earth facing the Sun is in DAYTIME. The side of the Earth facing away from the Sun is in NIGHT-TIME.]

3 365 and a quarter. A year.

4 The Earth's axis is tilted so each hemisphere is sometimes tilted towards the Sun (long days and short nights) and sometimes away (short days and long nights).

5 Collision between Earth and another planet about the size of Mars about 4.5 billion years ago.

6 Light from the Sun is reflected off the surface to our eyes.

Exercise 8.4b

1 atmosphere

2 two-thirds

3 axis, light, darkness

4 24 hours, axis, day

5 365 and a quarter, year

6 sphere

7 28 days

8 non-luminous, reflected

9 Forces

This chapter covers the following elements of the National Curriculum for Year 5.

Pupils should be taught to:

- explain that unsupported objects fall towards the Earth because of the force of gravity acting between the Earth and the falling object
- identify the effects of air resistance, water resistance and friction that act between moving surfaces
- recognise that some mechanisms, including levers, pulleys and gears, allow a smaller force to have a greater effect.

It also covers the following elements not mentioned in the National Curriculum

Pupils should be taught:

- that when objects (for example, a spring, a table) are pushed or pulled, an opposing pull or push can be felt (ISEB 5b)
- that the unit of force is the newton and that forces can be measured using a force meter (newton meter) (ISEB 5a)
- how to measure and identify the direction in which forces act (ISEB 5c).

Activities in this chapter offer opportunities to work scientifically by:

- making observations
- making accurate measurement using appropriate equipment
- recording and reporting findings and observations in a variety of formats, including diagrams, tables, charts and graphs.

Exercise 9.1

1 pull, push, twist

2 direction, speed

3 friction

4 pull

5 gravitational

6 increase, reduces

Exercise 9.2a

1 able to return to its original size/shape when compressed or stretched

2 If the spring is extended too far it will pass its elastic limit, which means it will not return to its original length. The force meter will then be inaccurate.

3 (a) Support/reaction force from the table supports it/is in balance with the gravitational force.

   (b) The ice cannot make a strong enough support force to balance the downward force (weight) of the person walking on the ice (especially as all the weight is concentrated into the small area of the feet).

4 upthrust

5 Downward force of canoe due to gravity (weight) is balanced by an equal upward force from the water.

6 Heavy boots increase downward force until it is greater than the possible upthrust force, so the diver sinks.

Exercise 9.2b: extension

Nail has very small surface area for upthrust to work on. Ship has a much larger surface area relative to its downward gravitational force (weight) and so there is a lot of water underneath to support it. (Note: Concept of density is covered in Y7/8).

Exercise 9.3

1 force magnifier

2 fulcrum or pivot

3 long

4 Effort needed to lift loads is applied downwards rather than upwards and this is easier.

5 block and tackle

6 a gear is a wheel with teeth all round its rim

7 bicycle wheels/chain, car engine (accept any valid suggestion)

Exercise 9.4

1 arrows

2 direction

3 length

4 equal

5 longer

6 tail

7 gravity